I0164425

FINDING FIDO
Practical Steps for
Finding Your Lost Pet

C.A.Wulff
With Annie Aaron Weddle

Barking Planet Productions

Marblehead, Massachusetts

**Finding Fido; Practical Steps for
Finding Your Lost Pet**
A service from Lost & Found Ohio Pets

ISBN
0-9786928-7-X
978-09786928-7-2

All proceeds benefit
The Beagle Freedom Project

Photograph of Lanie used by permission.

Barking Planet Productions
Marblehead, Massachusetts

Author's Note:

Because the Internet is constantly changing, I cannot guarantee that the websites listed in this book will be active indefinitely. My hope is to update this guide as changes and growth warrant.

If you are part of a rescue group and would like to offer this guide for free download on your website, contact me on my Facebook author page: C.A.Wulff [https://www.facebook.com/pages/CAWulff/156898 504349943?ref=ts&fref=ts]

Acknowledgments:

Sincere thanks to my co-administrators on the Lost & Found Ohio Pets Facebook page: Annie Aaron Weddle and Karen Muehlenhard Flake. Annie and Karen devote hours of their time helping keep the page up to date and networking the animals to pounds and humane societies across the state. They work tirelessly to give misplaced Ohio pets the best chances of getting back to their families.

Also, my sincere appreciation to the many repeat visitors to the page, who help us disseminate the information about misplaced pets throughout their own networks.

Special appreciation to Annie for helping with the tips found in this guide.

Thanks, also, to Robert & Stella McCarty of Barking Planet Productions for their support and encouragement in bringing this guide to fruition.

Losing a pet is a harrowing and stressful experience. **Lost & Found Ohio Pets** [www.facebook.com/ LostFoundOhioPets] offers this guide as a service to pet guardians in hopes that it will help prevent the loss of a pet, or assist in finding a lost pet.

Some statistics:
- 1 in 3 pets will be lost at some time during their life.
- Only 22% of lost pets will be reunited with their owners
- 52% of microchipped pets are reunited with their owners.

Because we have noticed the number of beagles that are lost and that fill our nation's pounds, all of the proceeds from the sale of this book will benefit The Beagle Freedom Project.

Finding Fido

Table of Contents

INTRODUCTION
A few words about lost pets and the dangerous findings that motivated me.

My mom used to say *"No good deed goes unpunished."* I never understood that to its fullest extent until now.

In March of 2013 I got this "great idea" to start a Lost & Found pets page on Facebook. I've been wanting to do a Lost & Found service of some kind for years...since two of our dogs went missing in the '90's. Back then, although we'd found one of our dogs right away, the other one was gone almost two weeks, and it was a very stressful experience trying to find her. Starting a page on Facebook seemed perfect to me because of the ease of networking. Facebook really lends itself to a project like Lost & Found animals.

I'd already been sharing animals to a national L&F page, when the idea occurred to me. I thought a page focusing on animals in a single area would be better than a nationwide page. I searched for an Ohio Lost & Found pets page and didn't find one, so I recruited my friend, Annie, and went ahead and set one up. (I have since discovered that just because I didn't find one, didn't mean that a number of them don't already exist...I just hadn't searched the right keywords. There is an Ohio Lost & Found Pet Portal and there are also a number of pages that are county specific.)

But, anyway, I didn't know that, so Lost & Found Ohio Pets was born.

LOST & FOUND
OHIO PETS

Lost & Found Ohio Pets

The page caught on right away, and within a week we were reaching 11,000 people, even though only 300+ had liked the page. People were sharing and cross-posting with the other Ohio Lost and Found pages.

After about two weeks, certain things began becoming clear to me...things I found disturbing. The first being: all those lost pets? Where do they end up?

- In some cases – like the spate of disappearances / thefts in 2013 of pets in Dayton, Ohio – they end up the victims of dog fighters who are blooding their fighting dogs.

- In some cases, they get hit by cars.

- In some cases, they are found by people in the community...but those people generally can't hang onto a dog for an extended period while they try to find the owner. They end up turning the animal over to their local animal control or humane society.

- In some cases, they are picked up directly by animal control in a neighboring community.

For now, I just want to discuss the last two scenarios. *The lost pets that end up in shelters and pounds.*

One afternoon I was calling people who had posted FOUND dogs to my page to see if they still had the dog or if they had found the owner, and the majority of them had turned the pet over to local animal control. One case was a pug, and I was anxious to find out if the finder still had him, because someone had just posted a lost pug on the Lost & Found Ohio Pets page. When I called, I got a voice mail recording that said the pug had been turned over to Summit County Animal Control on Opportunity Parkway. (The fact that the Akron pound is on a road called "Opportunity Parkway" seems like an ironic and sick joke, given the pound's history. However, the Akron Beacon Journal recently reported that the pound is much improved since those days of scandal.) I called Summit County Animal Control after finding this out, and asked about the pug who had been brought in. The man who answered the phone looked at his impound list. He said "We haven't had any pugs come in."

I asked him to double check. I asked him to look back a couple of days. He replied something like this: *"On Friday we got a pit bull, a pit bull, a shepherd mix, a pit bull and a terrier. On Saturday we got a Pomeranian, a pit bull, a pit bull, a terrier and a Jack Russell. Oh wait...on Thursday, last Thursday, we got a pug. It's been adopted out."*
This conversation rattled me for a couple of different reasons.

- First, Summit AC has a dubious record.

- Secondly...he had said 'no pug' and had to be asked to look back further, even though I gave him a target date when I called. What if that was my dog? What if he'd said "no pug" and I said "OK, thanks" and hung up?

- Thirdly – that seemed like a lot of animals impounded in just a couple of days, and awfully generic.

- Fourth – the pug had already been adopted out...so if that dog's owner was searching for him, he was no longer stray, and no longer impounded. No longer *findable*.

- Fifth – I knew that **all** of the pets there, all of the ones on his list were in imminent danger of being killed, and that some of them, maybe the *majority* of them, were lost pets.

Now, in advocacy, there are certain things I know. Shelter statistics dance across my desk on a regular basis, and that particular week, I'd seen a lot of them. Practically every place I had turned, there was a new shelter statistic assaulting my senses.

- *33%-45% of pit bulls end up in a shelter at some point in their lives.*
- *75% of them are killed.(the day I called, the Summit AC had rattled off at least 5 they'd impounded in the past two days.)*
- *The Adrion W Baird Animal Center in Campbell County Tennessee kills 95% of the animals that come through their doors.*
- *Robeson County Animal Shelter in NC has a 90% kill rate.*
- *Montgomery County Animal Shelter in NC has a 99% kill rate! Last year they killed 100 percent of the cats and 98 percent of the dogs that came into their facility.*
- *PETA kills 96% of the animals that enter their Norfolk Virginia shelter.*

- *Between 3 and 4 million shelter animals are killed **every year** in the United States. That's 456 animals per hour, or more than 7 animals per minute. It's more than the combined total human population of North Dakota, South Dakota, West Virginia, and Wyoming!*

I'm in Ohio, and my Lost & Found page is for *Ohio pets*...but Ohio shelters don't do any better than those shelters in Tennessee, North Carolina, Virginia, or anywhere else in the country.

My "great idea" had just gotten a whole lot more complicated...because now it was clear to me that I needed to make sure that the lost pets on my page got shared to – and alerted – all the animal control facilities in the county where the pet has gone missing as well as surrounding counties.

And in addition to that realization, I also came to understand that a lot of pet owners are so upset when they lose their pet, that they don't know what to do. They might post that the pet is lost, but they don't always include vital information like whether or not the animal is male or female, or a phone number where they can be reached! Most pet owners don't know that if your pet is missing, you **have** to go to the shelter in person. You cannot rely on the person who answers the phone when you call.

And these realizations mean that I needed to give pet owners the tools to find their lost animals!

So I began devoting my Friday *Cleveland Pets Examiner* column to writing a Lost & Found Friday article that gives tips for finding lost pets...and once I had a bunch of information, it only seemed logical to compile it all together into a manual of sorts.
So here you go. I hope it's helpful. Please share the link where you downloaded it with others so they can download it too.

And **PLEASE**, be responsible. License your dogs. Make sure they have ID. Microchip them. Spay and Neuter them. Don't leave them unattended outdoors or in cars. Don't tie them out and walk away thinking they are safe. Their safety is in your hands.

Finding Fido

Chapter 1

BEFORE YOU LOSE A PET

Prevention: lower the risk of losing your pet
If you compare a cross section of lost pets, you will find that there are certain factors that account for the majority of missing pets. The two most common types of pets who run off are ones that are not spayed or neutered and ones that have recently been adopted from a shelter or rescue.

Intact pets (those that are not spayed or neutered) run off to answer the call of nature. A male dog can smell a female dog in heat for miles, and he will take the first opportunity to get out of his house or yard to satisfy his urge to mate with her. You can eliminate this risk completely by having your pet spayed or neutered.

Spaying and neutering is part of responsible pet ownership. It keeps your pet safe by eliminating their urge to roam, but it also has many other benefits. Altered pets have a much lower chance of acquiring testicular or mammary cancer, or Pyometra, [http://en.wikipedia.org/wiki/Pyometra] are better behaved, and do not mark territory. Spaying and neutering also saves lives by preventing unwanted litters of puppies and kittens.

Pets that have just been adopted from a rescue or shelter are at high risk to be runners. Although they can't tell us why, if we look at what they've just been through, it is possible to make a pretty good guess. Shelters and rescues are full of animals who were picked up by animal control or surrendered by owners. Shelters are loud and confusing places for a pet who is already feeling disoriented. The pets there are probably all wondering where their families are and how to get back to them. That's why at the first chance, a newly adopted pet might take off; hoping to find his lost family.

Transition

When you are bringing home a newly adopted pet, you have to allow for a ***transition period.*** Immediately leash-walk your new dog around your neighborhood so he can take in the smells and sounds of his new environment and orient himself. Pick a special place and encourage him to potty there. Be consistent. When you take him in the house, keep him on the leash to show him around. Be calm and confident so he knows you are in charge and so he will feel safe. Take him outside to the yard for a short time and back into the house, keeping a leash on him at all times. If possible, install a baby gate near the door you use to go in and out, for a little extra security.

Remember, your new pet will be excited and anxious about his new home. Give him time and space to get settled and try to resist overwhelming him with attention at first. Make sure that doors and gates are securely closed and that he is not allowed outdoors without a leash for the first few weeks -- even if your yard is fenced. When you are finally ready to let him have the run of the fenced back yard, make sure there are no gaps, and that all boards are secure.

Practical steps for how to avoid losing your pet

1. Spay or neuter your pet. I'm repeating this because of the huge difference it makes! Believe it or not, 8 out of 10 animals listed on the Lost & Found Ohio Pets Facebook page are unaltered animals. It's a fact that pets that are not spayed or neutered are much more likely to roam or run away. They want to answer the call of nature: but in a country where 4 million healthy animals are killed in shelters every year, it is simply irresponsible not to spay/neuter.

2. Don't let your pet roam. Most cities and towns have leash laws – *follow* them. Make sure your yard is secure so your pet can't escape. When you are out of doors, have your pet on a leash and in your control.

3. Never leave your pet unattended in the yard or in the car. Leaving a pet unattended makes her an easy target for thieves. People who steal pets don't normally steal them because they want to keep them. They steal them to make money from them. Stolen pets might be bred, sold to class B dealers who sell them to laboratories, sold for profit, or used to blood fighting dogs. Don't let your pet be an easy target – her safety is your responsibility!

4. Don't talk about your pet's financial value with strangers. *Do* tell them your pet means the world to you.

5. Microchip your pet. (more information on microchipping and its benefits follows this section.) A microchip is about the size of a grain of rice and it is inserted under the pet's skin. Many rescue organizations and veterinarians will microchip your pet for you. The chip is registered with an ID number and if your pet goes missing, she can be scanned by animal control to find out where she belongs.

6. Your pet should have a collar with an identification tag* and a license. This is not as effective as microchipping, because a lost pet can get snagged by the collar and slip out of it. A collar can come loose. Tags can fall off. Tags can become unreadable. The information on them can become obsolete if you move or change your phone number. Always make sure your pet's tags are readable and that they list two phone numbers (with area code!) An address is also good, but is not as important as phone numbers, it's more important that the person who finds your pet can reach you by phone immediately. If your dog has a lot of tags that rub against each other and compromise the engraving,

purchase a collar with the phone number printed or woven into it. License your dog in your county! It's the law in many states and sometimes it is a pet's ticket home!

7. Invest in good fences, good gates, good windows, doors, and latches.

8. Teach your dog the "STOP" command. This is invaluable any time she is off leash – to prevent her chasing any stimulus that appeals to her prey drive.

9. If your dog's neck is bigger than her head (like a greyhound), or if your dog slips her collar, buy a Martingale collar. These collars have two loops instead of one, designed to prevent dogs from easily slipping out of their collars. It tightens without cutting off the dog's airway as choker chains do.

10. Take pictures of your pets. If you regularly groom your pet, have before and after photos. A pet that's lost for any length of time will not look newly groomed for long. Know where you have the photos stored so if you have to make LOST posters you'll have them.

11. ID bands are a common method of tagging and labeling various kinds of birds. Your bird may already have an ID band, especially if you have bought the bird from a breeder, or if it was imported. Make sure you know the numbers on your bird's tag so you can

provide that information. You can also photograph the unique skin patterns on your bird's feet – it is much like fingerprinting a human as every bird's pattern is unique.

Microchipping

One of the best ways to ensure that your pet will find her way home if she ever becomes lost is by microchipping her. A microchip is a permanent identification system. Even though your pet may have identification tags, anything can happen while she is on the run. Tags can get snagged and fall off, collars can be lost. But a microchip implant is a surefire permanent identification method.

A microchip is no bigger than a grain of rice. Veterinarians or a rescue group can implant the chips into all kinds of pets -- from reptiles and birds to cats and dogs. The device carries a number, and that number is attached to a database that includes the name and contact information of a pet's owner. When a pet is picked up by a rescue or animal control, one of the first things they do is scan the pet for a microchip. Since almost 4 million animals are killed in shelters each year, and since many of them are lost pets, a microchip could save your lost pet's life.

AVID and HomeAgain are the largest sellers of pet microchips. AVID reports that their microchips help reunite as many as 1,400 pets with their owners every day, and HomeAgain boasts a total of more than 400,000 pet recoveries [source: www.avidplc.com].

HomeAgain also offers a free app called Petrescuers for its members. The app is free and accesses a large network of other pet owners and dog lovers whom are contacted in the case of a lost companion. You can post lost dogs on their forums and dog related sites.

Here's an article that explains exactly how a microchip works: http://science.howstuffworks.com/innovation/everyday-innovations/pet-microchip1.htm

A hypodermic needle is used to implant a microchip, and the pet only feels about the same discomfort she feels when she is vaccinated. Microchipping costs about $25.00, but sometimes rescue groups offer discounts at adoption events. After your pet is microchipped, she needs to be registered with the manufacturer of the device.

When you register, you provide the identification number and your contact information or your veterinarian's contact information. When a shelter finds your pet, they use scanners to read the number and contact an agency that manages the database. The agency then contacts you with the good news that your lost pet has been found. It's important you keep your contact information up-to-date in the database. Whenever you move or get a new phone number or email address, you should notify the agency of the change immediately.

QR ID TAGS

Technology and convention have collided to create a new type of ID tag. The QR (Quick Response) ID tag takes conventional ID tags up a notch and may be a good alternative to microchipping – or it can be a back-up to be used along with the microchip for extra protection against loss. Like other tags, it can be lost, but the advantage of the tag is that anyone with a Smartphone can scan it, so there is no need to take a found dog to a vet or shelter to be scanned for a chip.

These tags have a QR code on them; those funny little black and white square codes that can be scanned with a Smartphone to access a host of information. They help to quickly and positively identify your pet unlike other tags. Conventional tags only allow so many characters for information like pet's name, address and phone number. On QR tags, the information is not limited to what is physically on a tag. Each tag has its own web address where you control the information. You can include multiple contact numbers, information about your pet's health, vet contact and more. You decide what information you want to be visible.

A QR tag allows you to update your pet's info from anywhere, and they have a web address on the back so someone without a Smartphone can still access the information via computer or tablet. There are several companies selling the QR tags.

FurCode. [www.furcode.com/] If your dog's tags are always rubbing, FurCode also offers collars with slide on QR codes.

PetQRTag.[petqrtag.com/] This company offers several different tag shapes.

QRPet Tracker. [qrpet.net] This company offers GPS tracking with their tag, so you will receive approximate GPS coordinates and a Google Map link of where your pet's QR tag was scanned. This service is free for one year, and then renewable with a small fee for each additional year.

There are other companies who sell the tags in various materials and shapes. A Google search will give you several to choose from.

Finding Fido

Chapter 2

IF YOUR PET GETS LOOSE

DOGS: Catching a dog that gets loose

If your dog gets loose, or if you are trying to catch a loose dog, DO NOT CHASE him. Dogs view that as a game. Instead, try this: get the dog's attention with voice or noise, and when the dog looks at you, sit or lie down on the ground and do your best imitation of inviting the dog to play. Most dogs cannot resist this and will come to you.

When you have the dog back in your control, DO NOT SCOLD or punish. Praise the dog for coming to you.

CATS: Catching a cat that gets loose

If your indoor cat gets loose it can be a strange and disorienting experience for him. The smells and sounds of being outdoors will be intoxicating, but he may still be quite frightened and want to stay hidden. Go out in the yard during a quiet time and call him softly, listening for meows in answer. Try to pinpoint where in the yard he is hiding. Once you have a location, you can try luring him out from his hiding place with a favorite toy on a string. Should that fail, try shaking the box of cat food out in the yard so it makes the familiar 'feeding time' sound. If your cat comes out of hiding, walk toward the house giving the box a little shake as you go to entice your cat to follow. Sometimes the can opener does magic; crack the door open and make the familiar can opener sounds just inside the door.

If you do not have luck with any of these methods, call your local animal control and ask if they have a humane trap (sometimes called a "live" trap) you can borrow. Place the trap in the area where you have seen him but not out in the open, try under some bushes or alongside the house. Bait it with your cat's favorite treat or food; smelly food (like tuna) works best. If you do catch your cat in the trap, cover it with a towel and carry it into the house before you try to take him out of it.

BIRDS: Catching a bird that gets loose

The best way to avoid a pet bird getting loose is to make sure to keep doors and windows secured when she is out of her cage, and keep her wings clipped. Any vet can help you with that procedure. If your pet bird escapes, there are some tips for recovering her.

Act quickly, the faster you react – the better. Scan trees and other obvious perches on your property and surrounding properties. If you can see your bird, and get her to see you, she may actually fly back to you. In some cases a bird may be in shock or be too afraid to move very much. In those instances, be sure to keep a close eye on the bird as you try to work out a plan for her retrieval. Maintaining visual contact is very important for the best chances of getting your bird back. Stay calm and confident. Many people give up too soon.

Put her cage outdoors and leave the cage door open. Many times a pet bird will return to her cage if she can see it, because it represents comfort and security. Put some of your bird's favorite treats in and around the cage.

Call your bird: remain close to where she is and repeat familiar words, sounds, and phrases. In some instances, it may entice your pet to fly down to you.

Morning and late afternoon/evening are the most likely times that the bird will come to you.

If you have a second bird that the lost bird will recognize the calls from, put the second bird outside (in a cage!) where the bird can hear it. Remember, don't leave any caged bird outside unattended, it makes them vulnerable to predators.

If the bird has been out for a while, have a picnic right under the tree where the bird is. Make sure it's something tempting, like French fries. Make a big deal about how delicious it is.

If you lose sight of your bird, follow the steps in the rest of this guide for creating and posting flyers and for networking your lost pet. Be sure to contact vets, pet stores and humane societies as far away as 50 miles.

Chapter 3

WHEN YOUR PET GOES MISSING

Why you need to go to the pound in person.

If your pet is lost, one of your first instincts will be to call your local animal control or humane society. Calling is OK for getting word to them that you are looking for a lost pet, but if you are calling to see if your pet is there, you can't rely on what you are told over the phone. Too many pounds will not even look at the animals in their kennels when you call.

Your pet may not yet be listed in the records at the front desk, and the way you describe your pet may not be the way a shelter would describe your pet. Any animal may become dirty, matted and neglected looking very quickly. It cannot be stressed enough *you must visit the shelter in person*, even if your pet was wearing tags when he was lost.

You will need to go to the shelters at least every other day. Few shelters can keep animals for more than 72 hours. Sometimes it takes more than a few days for a pet to be picked up and brought to a shelter.

It's important that you check all the shelters within 20 miles of where your pet was lost. In many areas stray animals are picked up by a government agency which holds them for a period and then turns them over to a shelter. If someone took your pet in for a few days hoping you would knock on their door and ask about it, they might later drop your pet off at the shelter that's most convenient for them, which may not be the one closest to you.

Take a photo of your pet, or make flyers and take them with you. Ask to see the animals if possible. Provide a photo or flyer for animal control to keep while your pet is missing. Be sure to put your contact information on the photo/flyer.

Remember to check special hold areas

A lot of the pounds and animal control facilities now have a separate area for animals considered dangerous. If the dog you have lost is a pit bull or a bully breed look-alike (such as a boxer or mastiff, or Rottweiler or mix) your pet may be held in a separate area. Ask to see this area, so you can be sure your pet is not there. Too often, pets are killed because they are unclaimed, and you can't claim your pet unless you find her.

Even if your pet is as sweet and docile as can be, remember that the pound is a scary and confusing place, and many dogs bite or growl out of fear. A normally happy and well-adjusted pet can find herself in the special hold area if she shows even the least bit of aggression.

City and County run pounds will often kill animals to free up space. That doesn't mean that they wait to run out of room; it means that they kill animals in the shelter to make room 'just in case' they need the cages for the next stray. Some pounds are so full they may not even be able to identify your pet if it is there. *You must physically go to the pounds yourself to look.*

Standard operating procedure is to keep stray animals for 3 days. This is called a 'stray hold' and is meant to afford a pet's owner the chance to find their lost pet at the pound. After three days, all bets are off. If your animal has been injured or is sick, they will be first on the list to kill. If your animal is a pit bull, a boxer, a mastiff, a cane corso, a chow, or any breed resembling these, your pet may be killed immediately after stray hold just for the way she looks. Many pounds have rules against adopting out dogs that fit those descriptions.

If you have lost a cat, you need to know that pounds are so full of cats that 80-85% of them are killed. If for any reason your pet is considered 'unadoptable' by the pound, it will be killed; that reason could be anything from exhibiting fearful or aggressive behavior to being 'too old'.

Be vigilant!

Check the lost and found ads in your local paper daily. Check the lost & found ads and pet ads for your area on Craigslist. Check with local veterinarian offices a couple of times a week to see if anyone has brought in a 'new pet' that fits the description of the pet you are missing. Watch for 'found' ads in public places like your grocery store and pet store.

Getting the word out.

Two of the most important tools for finding your lost pet are flyers (LOST posters) and the Internet.

A few words about LOST posters:
You need to make effective signs to hang in your neighborhood.

When you are making a LOST poster, use the best photo of your pet that you have. Your pet's markings and colorings should be clearly visible. Make the photo as large as possible on the paper...use up almost the whole sheet. The less you write, the better; that way, the words can be larger. Include the date the pet went missing, the pet's name and gender, a description, and a contact number.

Here is a poster to use as a guide.

LOST

6/7 Lost Ellsworth, Oh
Rt 45/224
Female "Lanie" red
invsbl fence collar
Any info 330-555-5555

When placing your posters, work outward from your home in every direction for a two mile radius. The first place to start with a lost poster is right in your own yard. Make a sign for your front yard and attach the poster to it. That way, if anyone in your neighborhood sees your pet, they know which house the pet is missing from.

Flyers can be hung in a variety of local establishments. If you ask management, they are almost always willing to let you post a flyer of your lost pet. Think in terms of audience: you'll want to post in places where people are tuned into pets, like veterinarian offices and pet stores, and you will also want to post in places that get a lot of public traffic, such as gas stations, grocery stores, and restaurants. You will also want to make sure your local animal control, humane society, SPCA, or rescue group has a copy.

Ask businesses to put your fliers up in their break rooms. Be sure to canvas all the local drive-thru restaurants and bank tellers. Ask for the manager and ask them if you can leave some fliers for their break room and to keep them by the drive-thru window. Ask if you can post your flyer outside along the drive-through lane.

Hang a flyer in the windows of your car on each side, or write your message on your rear window with window paint markers. You'll reach a lot of people that way as you go about your day. Keep the information simple and to no more than 4 lines, so it can be written large enough for other drivers to see.

Make sure that the flyers you make and hang are effective. *Always include a photo* - in color if possible – and make sure it is a clear photo that shows any distinguishing characteristics your pet may have. Be sure to include the date your pet went missing, and the general location; more than one way to contact you; and any description to help identify your pet.

Put your flyers in prominent places; near doorways, on poles or trees at intersections, etc.

You will also want to call a lost ad into your local newspapers. Many offer this service at a low rate or free.

Post your pet's information and photo on the Internet. Many people use Craigslist.com to advertise their lost pets, and many use social media like Facebook.com. Sharing your lost pet on Facebook can get the information out to thousands of people. Look for your county animal control, humane society or SPCA online and post your pet's picture and information to their page or site. (but don't forget to notify them if your pet is found!) Type the words "Lost pet" into the Facebook search bar to find pages devoted to lost pet notices.

Lost & Found Ohio Pets has now designated a folder on their Facebook page for you to upload a lost poster of your pet. They urge you to save a copy of your poster as a .jpg or a .pdf and upload it. Making your lost poster available for download makes it accessible to others in your area, who may want to print it out and post signs in the neighborhood to help you.

Consider printing your lost poster on a T-shirt.

Wearing a LOST t-shirt while you run errands makes you a walking billboard for your lost pet. Ask your friends and family to participate, and if you're able, offer LOST poster T-shirts to kids in the neighborhood.

There are websites and photo stores that can make shirts for you, or if you have an ink jet printer, you can pick up a package of T-shirt iron-on paper and make your own transfers. Remember to flip the image and print it backwards, so when you iron it on your shirt, it will read correctly! Use the most attractive photo you can find of your pet to draw peoples' attention. Wearing a LOST t-shirt while you run errands makes you a walking billboard for your lost pet.

Ask your friends and family to participate, and if you're able, offer LOST poster t-shirts to kids in the neighborhood.

Provide an Accurate Description

If your pet goes missing, in addition to sharing his photo on social media sites and making and hanging LOST posters of him in your neighborhood, you will be making phone calls to local rescues, vets, police stations, and your local paper. This is why it is important for you to be able to describe your pet accurately.

That might seem like a no-brainer; we all know what our pets look like, but you need to know how to make someone who has never seen him able to recognize him. Think about your pet right now; without looking at him, see if you can describe him. What type of words did you use? Did you say he was "big" or "small"? Did you say how long his fur is? Did you say what color? Did you use a breed to describe him?

If your pet is a commonly known breed, that might be helpful. Almost everyone knows what a tabby cat is, or what a poodle or German Shepherd looks like. But if your dog is a less commonly known breed, such as a Cavalier King Charles Spaniel, or an English Setter, the majority of people will not know the characteristics of that breed. Be very, very specific in your description.

Instead of saying your dog is big, small, or medium sized, use a weight or measurement. If your pet is mostly white with colored spots, say where the spots are. Is your pet overweight? Is your pet on the thin side? Do ears stand up, or fold over? Take all of those characteristics into consideration. Most importantly, try to think of a distinguishing characteristic. Does your dog have blue eyes? A curled tail? No tail? Does your cat have a spot that is shaped like a heart? Does your pet have any scars or blemishes? Try to think of something unique.
Consider the following descriptions as an example.

- *Don't*: Large black and brown dog. Wearing a blue collar.

- *Do*: 85 pound dog. Short black fur. Brown legs, snout and eyebrows. Bob tail. Blue collar.

- *Don't*: Black and white cat

- *Do*: Fat black cat with white paws and face. Black mustache. Pink nose with black speck.

Which descriptions create a clearer picture?
Write a description of your pet and keep it with a good photo in case he ever gets lost.

Give your pet the best chance of being reunited with you.

There are a number of basic mistakes that people make when they post a lost pet online.

One of the biggest mistakes is that pet owners are not specific enough about where the pet was lost. Many times they list a road or crossroad, but fail to say what city or county. It's not uncommon for a pet's guardian to totally skip the location when posting a lost pet.

Lost & Found Ohio Pets had a person say their pet was missing from "Warren". The pet owner meant Warren Rd. in Cleveland/Cuyahoga County. But the dog was networked with Trumbull County facilities, because "Warren" is an Ohio city in Trumbull County. The guardian had not been specific enough and the dog was networked 60 miles from home! Remember, people reading your plea for help don't know where you live – you have to tell them! *Be very specific.*

Another mistake is not giving a date when the pet went missing. A date helps networkers cross check shelters by intake date. If you lose your pet on May 17, and a pet matching that description is found at a shelter with an intake date of the May 14, networkers know it's not the same pet and can move on.

Also, you will not want to miss any tips or sighting of your lost pet. If you are posting your lost pet on Facebook, be sure to provide an email address or a phone number where you can be reached. If you provide only your Facebook profile page and someone tries to contact you who is not your Facebook friend, their message will route to your "other" folder, where you might easily miss it.

Make the most out of Internet networking.

Lost & Found Ohio Pets reports that their Facebook page has less than 700 'likes', yet some of the listings of lost and found pets on their page have received more than 21,000 views! This is an example of the magic of social networking. Depending on how you set your page security, sharing a pet on your Facebook page can reach scores more than just the friends on your list.

Lost & Found Ohio Pets network the pets on their page with county shelters, animal control facilities, humane societies, and other pages for lost & found pets. Every page has their own followers, so the more places you post your lost or found pet, the more people will see it.

There are dozens of Facebook pages for networking lost and found pets. Just type the words Lost & Found in the search bar and follow it with your state or city. The search results will give you some good places to start. There are also some Facebook pages that share lost pets from every state.

Lost & Found Ohio Pets will post missing/lost/stolen/found pets in OH and up to 50 miles into states bordering Ohio.
[https://www.facebook.com/LostFoundOhioPets]

Missing PETS of Butler & Surrounding Counties, OHIO will post missing/lost/ stolen/found pets in OH, KY, IN:
[http://www.facebook.com/missingourpets]

Bring Clarice Home (Clarice is still missing), posts missing pets from all states:
[http://www.facebook.com/BringClariceHomeFor Christmas]

Bring Mabel Home (Mabel has been found), posts missing pets from all states:

[http://www.facebook.com/BringMabelHome]

Search for Sassy supports the search for missing dogs in all states.
[https://www.facebook.com/SearchForSassy]

Cincinnati Pit Crew posts missing/lost/ stolen/found pit bulls in the Tri-State area OH, KY, IN:
[http://www.facebook.com/CincinnatiPitCrew]

Marley's list posts missing pets in Ohio and Northern Kentucky:
[http://www.facebook.com/MarleysList?ref=ts& fref=ts]

Missing Small Dog Alert posts missing/ lost/stolen/found small dogs from all states:
[http://www.facebook.com/MSDAlert?ref=ts&fref= ts]

Dog Missing/Pet Lost & Found Alert Group posts lost animals from all around the U.S.
[https://www.facebook.com/groups/198089680645 /?ref=br_tf]

Pets Lost, Found, Reunited posts lost animals from all around the U.S.
[http://www.facebook.com/groups/PetsLFR/]

Before They are Missing (proactive registry)
[http://www.facebook.com/BeforeTheyAreMissing_]

Try to post just one or two photos (start by posting one on your personal Facebook page if you have one – be sure to set the post's privacy settings for "public") and then share those original posts to the other sites and groups. That way, comments, sightings and contact info are centralized. It's also fewer places to notify once your pet is found.

There are also websites devoted to helping you find your lost pet. I do not endorse any of these sites, they are listed only for your convenience.

Lost Pet U.S.A. [http://www.lostpetusa.net/home] is a national database of lost and found pets. You can list the pet you have lost or found and search their database for a match. The site also offers an online template for making a lost poster, and resources for getting additional help in your area.

Get Me Home [http://getmehome.com] is operated by Merial, the company that manufactures Heartgard and Frontline medications. The site registers your pet with a unique number and enters the information into their database. The site also serves as an extra contact in case your pet goes missing.

The Center for Lost Pets
[http://thecenterforlostpets.com] is a free lost & found registry/database made possible by the Humane Society of the United States.

Pets911 [http://pets911.com] is a free registry/database for both lost and found pets. The site also offers mobile apps for your iOS phone and other devices.

Fido Finder [http://fidofinder.com] is a free registry and database for lost and found pets serving the United States, Canada, and the UK. Fido Finder emails you when a pet enters the system that matches your pet's description. Unfortunately, there doesn't seem to be a way to upload an actual photo of your pet to this site. The images are clip art images of various breeds.

America's National Lost & Found Pet Database [http:lostfoundpets.us] is a national pet registry. You can register a lost or found pet into their searchable database. The free listing stays in their database until you remove it. For a donation of any amount you can post a lost ad on their home page for seven days.

Lost My Doggie [http://lostmydoggie.com] is a lost pet recovery service that has both free and paid services. They provide free Pet Amber Alert notification and will post your lost or found pet notice. For a fee, they will professionally design a lost poster and mail it to shelters and pet businesses in your area.

Pet Amber Alert [http://petamberalert.com] is a service that helps you get the word out. They have three paid plans, each one providing a different set of services, from creating lost posters for you to calling and faxing thousands of people and businesses at once.

HelpmefindMYPET [http://helpmefindmypet.com/] International ID registry will permanently register all of your pet's IDs including pet microchips, rabies tags, municipal tags and tattoo numbers in a North American Microchip Registration Database and Lost Pet Network. If your pet does not have any form of ID helpmefind**MYPET** will assign a unique identifier to your pet which can be engraved onto a stainless steel ID tag with the rest of your pet's important recovery information. HMFMP ID and Pet Microchip Registry is a 24 hour lost pet service. It is also a pay service, with six plans to choose from.

Find Toto [http://findtoto.com] is a paid service that provides fast and targeted alerts, print-ready flyers, and social networking.

Pet Harbor [http://petharbor.com] is a useful website where you can search for your lost pet in area shelters and rescue facilities. You can sign up for daily email alerts from whichever shelters or rescues you specify. The site also offers a paid, lost animal postcard service, although the price is quite steep.

Chapter 4

BOOTS ON THE GROUND

Where to Look for Dogs:

Even if you've made and distributed LOST posters, visited local pounds, animal control centers, and local rescues searching for your lost pet, you are still going to want to search for your pet in your own neighborhood.

The first rule is to always carry a leash with you while you are looking! It also helps to have a pocket full of treats.

In order to know the best places to look, you need to think carefully about your pet's personality and other specifics. Is your pet afraid of loud noises? Does your pet love children? Is your pet unaltered and possibly looking to mate? Have you recently moved to the neighborhood, or is your pet new to your home?

According to Petfinder.com, if you are searching for a dog as soon as he escapes, a big strong dog can run five miles or more before tiring. Small dogs may only be able to run about a half a mile. They report that most dogs are found within a two mile circle of their home, because dogs don't normally run in a straight line. We all know how dogs like to sniff everything, so they tend to zig and zag to check out all the neat smells.

If your dog is friendly, and/or loves children, try checking in the local parks and schoolyards. Ask children you see in the neighborhood to keep on the lookout.

If your dog is highly motivated by food, follow your nose and find out who is barbecuing in the neighborhood.

If your dog is shy and doesn't trust strangers, check under cars and in quiet areas.

Don't forget to talk to people who travel through your neighborhood daily, like the paper boy, lawn services and the postman. Give them one of your lost flyers and ask them to watch out for your pet. They are your eyes on the ground.

The longer your pet is gone, the harder it will be to find him.

If your pet is gone for days, he has most likely tried to return home and failed. Any number of things might have happened. He could be hurt. He could have been picked up by animal control, or someone could have taken him in.

Believe it or not, odds are greater that someone has him in their home. Petfinder reports that 40% of households have pets, and people in those homes respond favorably to a lost pet. It might be someone driving by who had your dog get in their car. It might be someone who works in the neighborhood, but doesn't live there. Of course, once someone takes him out of your neighborhood, it becomes harder to find him.

Although we don't like to think about it, it makes sense to check with your city and speak with someone at the department in charge of removing dead animals. Let them know you are looking for a lost pet, and ask if you can check their list. Every time you check the list and don't find your pet, it fuels the hope to continue searching.

Some people who pick up a lost pet, even though they have good intentions, aren't equipped to hold onto a pet they've found, and they will take the animal to a vet, kennels, groomers, even pet stores. They take them to animal shelters (which are sometimes distant and have restricted operating hours) and to rescue organizations.

Be methodical, and be thorough.

Where to Look for Cats:

If you are really sure your cat has gone missing and is not hiding somewhere in the house taking a long nap, start with your own yard. Cats that are used to being kept indoors usually do not venture very far when they get out – it's too scary. They tend to hunker down someplace where they are hidden, but can still watch everything. If you call your cat while standing in your yard and you don't hear any answering meow, place the cat's scratching post, litter box or recently used bedding outside near your door. Cats use scent to identify a place as home, and these things will serve as a guide if your cat has gone into a neighbor's yard.

Put a baby monitor on your porch near a bowl of food. If your cat is hiding in the yard, she may stay hidden until everything is quiet in your neighborhood and not venture out of hiding until the wee hours of the morning. A baby monitor can alert you to her presence if she makes a late night or early morning visit.

Believe it or not, many cats who get to go outdoors regularly have more than one home and it's not unusual for two families to share a pet cat without even realizing it. This accounts for some of the cats that go missing, because one of the families may move, or arbitrarily decide one day to begin keeping the cat indoors all the time. Talk to people on your street, and hand out LOST flyers.

Has a neighbor moved during the time that coincides with your cat going missing? If so, contact them and ask if they have your cat. If you don't have a contact number for them, you may want to find out where they moved and send notices to the vets, newspapers and pet related businesses in that town. Write something like "Think my cat moved with a neighbor from _____ to _____".

If you don't know of any neighbors having moved recently, keep your cat's curiosity in mind. They love to explore new places. Many a cat has inadvertently been closed up in a neighbor's garage or shed for days or even weeks at a time with no one being the wiser. Walk your street late at night or very early in the morning when the neighborhood is quiet and call for your cat at the end of driveways. Listen closely for any answering meows.

Cats also sometimes get "accidentally abducted" by climbing into cars and moving trucks and being driven out of the neighborhood. Run a 'lost' ad in the newspaper – they are often free and can get the word out over an extensive distance.

Hang LOST posters around your neighborhood and be sure to check with your city and speak with someone at the department in charge of removing dead animals. Let them know you are looking for a lost pet, and ask if you can check their list. Every time you check the list and don't find your pet, it means there is hope your cat is still out there.

Don't give up hope! Many pets have been found weeks, and even *months*, after they've gone missing.

If you think your pet was stolen

If you have reason to believe that your pet has been stolen and has not just run off, be sure to file a report with the police. Keep records of your dog's financial value so that they will consider it theft of valuable property (police need a monetary value to report). This increases the chances they will pursue the subject.

Then follow all of the previous suggestions for finding a lost dog, but be sure to add "Stolen" or "Possibly Stolen" to your posters and online pleas.

Chapter 5

WHAT TO DO IF YOU FIND STRAY PET

Capture and contain the animal. (see how to catch a loose dog, cat or bird) Always approach stray animals slowly and cautiously while speaking in a calm, gentle voice. You can also use food to coax a frightened animal into approaching you.

Create a barrier or use a carrier, leash, piece of cloth, or length of rope to keep the animal from leaving the area. Signal approaching vehicles to slow down if you cannot confine the animal, or divert traffic around him if he appears to be injured and is still on the roadway.

Try to secure a dog in a fenced yard or on a leash. You can use a belt or piece of rope as a slip lead in an emergency, but once you've captured the dog, you'll have to do better than that.

When trying to catch a pet bird, cat, or other small pet, a sheet, blanket, or towel thrown on them can help stop the animal so you can pick it up. Most cats do not like to be restrained, so stray cats and other small animals are best confined inside a cat carrier, secure box (with air holes), small room of your house or temporarily in your car (as long as the car is well ventilated and not too hot).

Know the law Be sure to check the laws in your state. In Ohio, if someone "finds" an animal, *they are required by law* to notify the dog warden in their county. If the plan is to search for the owner of the animal, a **PUBLIC NOTICE** must be posted for **10 days**, after which time if the owners are not found, the "finder" may legally keep the animal as their own or rehome him.

Check the pet for ID. Once you have contained the lost pet, check to see if the animal is wearing an ID tag. If so, you may be able to immediately contact the owner and return the pet. If the pet is wearing ID, but you are unable to immediately make contact with the owner, try to hold onto the pet for a few hours and try again later, or wait for a call back from the owner. Call your local animal shelter and animal control to report that you've found the pet. Give them a good description and leave a contact number in case the owner calls or goes there to search for the pet.

Next, *don't panic*. Many people who find a lost pet are immediately overwhelmed because they have to come up with some fast solutions for a strange pet. Unfortunately, their first instinct is often to take the dog to their local pound.

Please take other solutions into consideration before relinquishing a stray pet to the pound. In most cases, stray pets are only afforded three days of safety at the pound. After that, they can be killed for any number of reasons. If they are frightened being at the pound, they can be deemed aggressive and unadoptable. If the facility is full, they can be killed to free up space. If there are particularly lazy shelter employees on duty, they may kill so they won't have to clean cages.

If you lost your pet, you'd want more than three days to find her, wouldn't you?

If you're uncertain about whether or not to help or keep an animal you see alongside the road, here's a final thing to consider: What would you want the finder of your lost animal to do if he happened to find him injured without his collar? Accidents can happen to anyone. The frantic owner could be looking everywhere for their pet.

If it were your pet, you'd want her to have veterinary help, and you'd want the finder to try to contact you. At the same time, be reasonable about how much you can afford to do for that animal if no owner shows up.

If the animal is injured or sick and dropped at the pound, the animal will most likely be killed right after the stray hold. Most pounds don't have the funds to vet sick and injured animals.

If you take an injured animal to a private veterinary hospital for treatment, you have to be willing to assume financial responsibility. Some vets have a special fund for emergencies, so be sure to ask.

Local rescues may be able to help by providing information about which veterinarians in the area are open for emergencies, and which ones may have the best prices. It's easy enough to find rescues in your area online by googling your city and state followed by the keywords "animal rescue".

Get the pet scanned for a microchip. If the pet is not wearing an ID tag, take the pet to the local animal shelter or a vet and have the pet scanned for a microchip. Some of the big box pet stores can scan too. If the animal is chipped, staff will be able to immediately look up the owner's contact information by calling the microchip company or accessing the microchip database online. ***It is absolutely essential that the animal be scanned for a microchip.***

Before taking the animal home, make sure you can keep your own pets separate; the found animal could be sick, fearful, or aggressive with other animals. Once you have him safely at your home, take pictures and create a "found pet" flyer to post around the area in which the animal was found. Unless you know for certain that the animal is a specific breed, describe the pet with as much detail as possible. Is the pet male or female? If he's male, is he neutered? What color is he? Does he have any distinguishing markings? How much does he weigh? Is he wearing a collar? You can post the LOST notices at veterinary hospitals, pet stores, restaurants, gas stations and ATM machines – wherever there is a lot of foot traffic. If you found the pet in your own neighborhood, go door to door with a photo of the animal and see if anyone knows who owns him.

Don't forget to list the found pet on web sites like those listed earlier in this guide. If you need support and direction, rescues can help you network the pet. Be sure to post a found report and photo on both the "Lost & Found" and "Pets" sections of www.craigslist.com for your city. You can also place a found ad in the classified section of your local newspaper (these are usually free).

If you've tried to find the owner without success, and are unable to keep the animal long-term, you can try to re-home the animal. Check with local animal rescue groups to see if they can help you. If you place an ad to rehome the animal yourself, NEVER offer the pet free! Free pet ads bring out the worst of the worst, and innocent pets very often fall into abusive hands and dangerous situations this way. Always ask a minimum of $35 to help ward off people who may have ulterior motives.

A New Home: Tips for rehoming a pet

If you do post an ad to find the pet a new home, be honest about the good and the bad. Disclose as much as you know about the pet, including whether or not she showed any aggression while you were caring for her, and whether or not she got along with other pets and/or children. Being honest will help ensure that you get quality responses from people who understand what they are taking on.

Always visit the home the pet is going to. Don't just hand the pet over to anyone who comes to your home and shows interest. Make sure they are who they say they are and have a home that is the right fit for the pet.

When finding a new home for a pet, you must be aware of the types of animal abuses and the potential for them. Always err on the side of safety. Never rehome an unaltered pet. There are low-cost spay/neuter programs in almost every major city. Rehoming an unaltered pet may land the animal with a backyard breeder. Go to the home the pet will be moving to. Make sure the pet is not ending up in hands of an animal hoarder. And never give a pet away for free. Asking a rehoming fee will help ensure she is not being taken for lab experiments or to be used as bait for a fighting dog.

Helping a homeless pet to find a new home is a rewarding experience. You can get more great tips and advice about rehoming an animal from the Sunbear Squad.
[http://www.sunbearsquad.org/how-to-find-a-new-home-for-your-pet.shtml]

Finding Fido

Epilogue

A PERSONAL STORY

In the 1990's when my partner and I lived in the city, we had a large fenced-in yard. We didn't know the dangers back then of leaving a pet unattended in the yard, and we learned the hard way. We left two of our four dogs, Pluto and Gypsy, in the yard while we left for a few hours. They had shade and water, but while we were gone they managed to get out of the gate and they were long gone by the time we got home.

This was in the days before everybody had a cell phone. I rushed in the house to grab some leashes and noticed the light on our answering machine blinking. There was a message from a neighbor on the next street who said Pluto and another dog had come by while they were barbecuing. The other dog had gone on, but Pluto had stayed for dinner. When they hadn't gotten a call back from us within an hour, they had called the city, and animal control had come by to pick Pluto up.

I contacted them immediately to thank them, and asked which direction the other dog had gone. Then I called the city and found out how to retrieve Pluto.

After we picked him up, we started canvassing the neighborhood for Gypsy, cruising the streets slowly and calling her name. There was no sign of her. When night fell, we went home and made a poster with her photo and contact information.

The next day, my partner and I each ran off dozens of posters at work, and that evening we hung them all over the neighborhood. We talked to anybody we saw in the yard or walking the streets near our home. A jogger told us he had seen Gypsy earlier that day.

For the next week, we searched for Gypsy every day from the time we got off work, until it got dark. We passed out flyers at our jobs. My partner gave flyers to every truck driver who came into her warehouse. We spoke to the mailman, and asked him to keep an eye out for our lost dog. We checked the paper every day. We called our local animal control. It was like she had vanished into thin air.

Gypsy had indeed vanished. She had found her way to our local Metropark, and she was having a great time. The Cleveland Metroparks stretch all across the city in a long string called "the Emerald Necklace". The park system covers some 22,000 acres in 18 adjoining reservations. Although we drove the parkway through the reservations near us, we never saw her.

Gypsy had been gone more than a week and the two of us were worried sick about her. We were barely eating and sleeping. To help us out, my partner's coworker, Bill, offered to hang flyers up on his way home from work one day. He had ridden his bicycle to work and would be covering about four miles on his way home. He took a stack of flyers with him and hung them along his route as he pedaled home.

A couple of hours later we got a call from Bill. It was like music to our ears when he said: "Come and get your dog."

Bill had made it home and was relaxing with a beer in front of the television when his wife asked him about the dog who was missing. Bill described Gypsy to her, and she pointed out their living room window. "Does it look like that dog?" she asked.

Gypsy was strolling past his house.

Bill wrenched open the door and called her name; when she turned to him, he knew it was Gypsy, and he caught her for us.

Gypsy had been gone for a week, but was less than five miles from home – she turned up on the other side of the Metropark reservation closest to us. And wow, did she ever smell bad! She must have been exploring the park the entire time, and rolled in raccoon dung or some other excrement. She was filthy and hungry; badly in need of a bath and a good meal.

Once she was bathed and fed, she slept for two straight days, and we had the best night's sleep we'd had in over a week, knowing our whole pack was safe and together again.

All of the proceeds from the sale of this book benefit
The Beagle Freedom Project.
http://www.beaglefreedomproject.org/

Beagle Freedom Project is a service of Animal Rescue, Media & Education (ARME). Founded in 2004, ARME is a nonprofit advocacy group created to eliminate the suffering of all animals through rescue, public education and outreach. ARME has found homes for thousands of homeless and abandoned animals. In 2004 ARME organized the first-ever "Shelter Drive" to provide creature comforts to homeless animals such as beds, toys and treats. ARME's Shelter Drive became an annual tradition uniting volunteers with businesses that allowed on-premise or on-site drop boxes for donations. ARME's compassionate army also helps feed and shelter displaced animals when Southern California fires strike residential areas.

ARME's **Beagle Freedom Project** (BFP) was formed in 2010 with the goal of rescuing research dogs (96% of whom are beagles) and as a vehicle to educate the general public about animal-testing, the importance of cruelty-free alternatives, and to advance legislative policy that will help end vivisection.

Over the course of 2012 and the first half of 2013 BFP has successfully liberated scores of "research" animals from laboratories across the world. Each one of these rescues brought significant and unquantifiable mainstream media attention to the plight of animals in laboratories. BFP has been featured in scores of television coverage, press stories, and online publications.

BFP has provoked a national conversation around the use of animals in laboratories via the exposure that the rescued beagles bring to the issue. Countless thousands of new supporters and compassionate consumers have been created from BFP campaigns, educational outreach events, and heart-breaking videos that consistently go viral and are social media sensations. The entire social media apparatus of BFP is dedicated to telling the stories of the rescued dogs and giving a face to actual victims of vivisection. The BFP Facebook page has 65k followers and several of the YouTube videos have gone viral reaching an audience of millions.

With the ultimate objective of ending animal-testing, BFP is amassing a new generation of anti-animal testing activists. These new advocates have been created with a carefully crafted message for mainstream America. 60 million U.S. households share their space and hearts with dogs, and there is no more quintessentially American breed than that of the beagle. The liberated laboratory beagles serve as the perfect ambassador to the general public, as they are instantly identifiable and easy to feel empathy with. The rescue of these dogs is a soft, but poignant, approach that can shock an otherwise animal-testing ignorant public into learning more and making pro-active lifestyle changes.

Beagle Freedom Project is pursuing a strategy unlike any other organization in the world and is having a remarkable effect in creating a new energy in opposition to animal-testing. BFP conducts inspiring rescue missions to educate the public to create support for pro-animal legislation!

RESCUES:

BFP conducts inspiring rescue missions to educate the public to create support for pro-animal legislation!

Since December 2010 Beagle Freedom Project has conducted 15 rescue missions that have saved 121 dogs (119 of which are beagles) from laboratories in every part of the U.S. and in addition to rescues in Spain and Albania. Beagle Freedom Project has also expanded and rescued 6 rabbits from 4 different laboratories and 2 cats from two others research facilities.

CAMPAIGNS:

In 2012 and 2013 a concerted effort has been made to expand the reach of BFP through a *50 State Campaign*. The most profound personal change comes through physical contact with these dogs. The public experiences their sweet nature, sees the tattooed ears and realizes animal-testing is not an abstract concept. The *50 State Campaign* aims to put a freed beagle in each state so these dogs can act as ambassadors in educational forums or media coverage. As of July 2013 BFP has 121 freed beagles in California, Oregon, Washington, Nevada, Arizona, Minnesota, Kentucky, Maryland, Washington DC, New York, New Hampshire, Maine, North Carolina, and Florida. From December 2012 to July 2013 BFP has coordinated over 100 outreach events and exposed tens of thousands to this cause.

To generate more rescues, BFP has written to every laboratory in the U.S. with dogs (383) asking for participation in the release program under the message that 'we owe them.' The *We Owe Them Campaign* was a spring 2013 online petition drive that has been shared and signed by 6,281 people across the U.S. It lets the public see the labs in their community, how many dogs are inside, and gives them a constructive outlet to protest. The **We Owe Them** concept has a universal appeal because it starts with a non-controversial premise that states *we owe these animals* after all they have suffered through in our name and they should have a chance at a life at the end of the experiment. This petition is the first point of engagement for many people whom have never taken a stand on an animal rights issue before, but feel inspired to do so here.

The Identity Campaign, launched by BFP in the spring of 2013, is a 'viral video' concept that captures public imagination, sparks online video participation, and generates media attention to the issue.

In laboratories across the U.S. and the world, dogs are only known by a Federal ID number tattooed in their ears. To highlight this historically relevant imagery and create a voice for these dogs, BFP has created temporary tattoos of the same design used on the beagles and with the actual number of one dog. Many supporters across the U.S. have put one on themselves and recorded a short video clip explaining their solidarity with nameless animals suffering in labs. Already this campaign has inspired creativity and the clips (or photos) are being "shared" on a variety of social media platforms. A social media meme that these dogs "have names and are not numbers" has taken hold and BFP is finalizing the construction of a website to host all of these videos at www.identitycampaign.org

LEGISLATION:

One of the most important projects of BFP over the last twelve months has been *the Beagle Freedom Bill*. Because the laboratories know exactly what BFP knows, that every freed beagle that enters the community lifts the secretive veil of animal-testing, most have become reluctant to free their "research animals", even if they are healthy and adoptable. In November of 2012, BFP proposed a legislative strategy that would alter the voluntary nature of laboratory animal release and instead, legally *compel* it. The idea is to mandate that research facilities that receive tax-dollar support would have to offer dogs and cats to non-profit rescue organizations for public adoption. From January to May of 2013 BFP ran this legislative campaign in the State of Minnesota. To support the bill BFP President Shannon Keith testified before the Senate Higher Education Finance committee about BFP, animal-testing, and the necessity of the new law. The bill passed the committee with unanimous support. Unfortunately the bill was ultimately killed behind the scenes under pressure from the lobbyists from the state University system.

Although unsuccessful in passing the legislation, the bill educated many law makers and brought public attention to the issue. For the next legislative session BFP will be advancing this same bill again in Minnesota, California and Michigan and far more vociferously.

To make a donation to the **Beagle Freedom Project**, visit: [https://beaglefreedomproject.nationbuilder. com/donate]

About the Authors

Cayr Ariel Wulff is an artist, author and animal advocate. She is a native Ohioan who has been involved in pet rescue for over twenty-five years. Wulff is a Contributing Editor at AnimalsVote.org; is the author of five non-fiction animal books; writes a pet column and an animal books column for Examiner.com and authors the blog "Up on the Woof". Currently, she resides in a log cabin deep in one of the Nation's National Parks with her lifemate and five dogs. She attributes her love of animals to having been raised by Wulffs.

The author's website: http://www.yelodoggie.com

Up on the Woof blog: http://thewoof.wordpress.com

Twitter feed: https://twitter.com/yelodoggie

Facebook page: C.A.Wulff

Annie Aaron Weddle is a business owner and animal advocate. She is a native Ohioan who has loved animals all her life. Wanting to follow in Jane Goodall's, footsteps, she studied Anthropology and Sociology in College. She has been a volunteer involved in animal rescue for more than a decade. Over the years she has shared her suburban home with dogs, cats, chickens & rabbits, – the majority of them rescues. Annie networks pets in pounds across the country in order to save their lives.

Annie's website:
https://www.facebook.com/pages/Once-Upon-A-Child-Stow-OH/129018740558364

Twitter feed: https://twitter.com/Ouacstowohio

Also by Cayr Ariel Wulff

Born Without a Tail (2007, BookSurge)
When your home has a revolving door for abused and abandoned animals, keeping pets takes on a whole new dimension!

Circling the Waggins: How 5 Misfit Dogs Saved Me from Bewilderness (2012, Barking Planet Productions)
More than twenty years of performing pet rescues could wear anyone down. Especially when the pets that end up being permanent residents in your home are the most irascible, insane and ridiculously unadoptable pets known to man.

Parade of Misfits (2013, Barking Planet Productions)
A mini-book of selections from the memoir "Circling the Waggins". Includes never before published essays about the author's dogs.

How to Change the World in 30 Seconds:
A Web Warrior's Guide to Animal Advocacy Online
(2013, Barking Planet Productions)
Combining case histories with practical tips, this guide demonstrates how to use the Internet to advocate for dogs; from simple clicks to more advanced methods.

What Readers have to say about:

HOW TO CHANGE THE WORLD IN 30 SECONDS

"Combining case histories with practical tips on how to use the Internet to advocate for dogs, Wulff's book is an inspiring, informative and highly useful volume that anyone who thinks dogs are worth fighting for should have on their shelf."
— John Woestendiek, author of *Dog, Inc.* & the website ohmidog!

"Social media will continue to change the way we live and work. This book helps animal advocates, regardless of one's experience level, keep up with that ever-changing landscape while making a true difference in the lives of these voiceless victims. Teeming with practical insights and filled with inspiration, How to Change the World in 30 Seconds is a must read for anybody who wants to engage in online animal advocacy."
— Scott A. Heiser, Sr. Attorney & Criminal Justice Program Director, Animal Legal Defense Fund

"It takes advocates and legislation to effect the way homeless animals live and die in the USA. We can stamp out this evil in our lifetime. This book will help you get started."
— Jackie Denton, National Director AnimalVotes.org, committed to ending shelter killing through issue-specific political activism.

CIRCLING THE WAGGINS

"There's a lot more to living with dogs than wet noses and going walkies. Cayr Ariel Wulff entertainingly chronicles the rocky flip side of pet care in **Circling the Waggins***, a heroic tale of triumph over turmoil and exhaustion. Wulff and her companion Dalene take in the misfits that have defeated lesser souls..."* - Bob Tarte, author of *Kitty Cornered, Enslaved by Ducks,* and *Fowl Weather.*

"Rescue people have some of the most extraordinary stories to tell and this book tells them well. The pain of loss and the unexpected beauties of life are shared in this book and I'm the richer for the reading." – S.L.Beardsley

PARADE OF MISFITS

"Parade of Misfits, aptly named, is an introduction -- an open door -- for dog lovers to the world of CA Wulff, author, passionate animal advocate, and dog lover. Living in a cabin in the woods with an ever changing melange of rescued canines and other critters, Wulff experienced a catharsis through her dogs. This book, propelled by humor and adventures, is a prelude to her full blown memoir, Circling the Waggins. The cover of the book is a true forecast of the world of Wulff you will find inside. – Robert McCarty, author of *Planet of the Dogs, Castle in the Mist,* and *Snow Valley Heroes.*

"This is a humorous introduction to the misfit pets of Wulff's memoir Circling the Waggins. This mini ebook is a sweet addition to the full book, containing two sample chapters and two previously unpublished essays - complete with hilarious full color photos of the author's quirky pack." – Carolyn Jourdan, author of *Medicine Men: Extreme Appalachian Doctoring,* and *Out on a Limb; a Smoky Mountain Mystery.*

BORN WITHOUT A TAIL

"Born Without a Tail captures the real scenario of those people who simply find it impossible to turn away, or say no to, a stray or an animal in need of human intervention and love. Wulff writes with an imagery that is easily visualized by the reader. Anyone who enjoys animals in the least will appreciate Wulff's adventures with these four-legged creatures." -- Brecksville Magazine

"Could not put it down. A very funny and touching look into the lives of rescuers. Any animal lover would love this book." – Gregory A. Schultz

Also from Barking Planet Productions

The *Planet of the Dog* Series
by Robert McCarty and Stella Mustanoja McCarty.

Long ago there were no dogs on planet earth...

Invaders threatened Green Valley...children were kidnapped
and taken to the Castle in the Mist...the King of the North
kidnapped two of Santa's reindeer...the people on Earth needed
help. These are the exhilarating stories of how dogs came down
from the Planet of the Dogs® to teach people about love,
loyalty, and courage – and to help bring peace to the land.

*Planet of the Dogs_* ISBN-13: 978-0978692803
Castle in the Mist ISBN-13: 978-0978692810
Snow Valley Heroes ISBN-13: 978-0978692827

Available from amazon.com and other retailers

What Readers have to say about:

The PLANET OF THE DOG Series

"I love this series of books and Planet of the Dogs sets the stage for those works that follow...This story borders between reality, a dream world, fantasy, fiction reality and wonderful imagination...The author has done a wonderful job of weaving this tale, making it a first rate fantasy read, while at the same time addressing quite real problems and indeed, how to fix those problems."
– Don Blankenship, Teacher, Editor/Reviewer at Good Books for Kids.

"Do you think it's possible for dogs to stop war? Author Robert J. McCarty has created a fantasy-allegory that can be read and understood on at least two different levels...a story about dogs who come from another planet to help people on earth. But under the surface are the important messages of friendship, love, loyalty, and how to overcome evil with good. Castle in the Mist will keep you turning the pages to find out what happens next."
– Wayne Walker, *Stories for Children Magazine*, *The Home School Book Review*, and *The Home School Buzz.*

"Any one of these books would make for a delightful – and one would assume, cherished gift for any child. All three would be an amazing reading adventure." – Darlene Arden, Educator, Dog Expert, author of *Small Dogs Big Hearts.*

Practical Steps for Finding Your Lost Pet

Practical Steps for Finding Your Lost Pet

Finding Fido

www.ingramcontent.com/pod-product-compliance
Lightning Source LLC
Chambersburg PA
CBHW070549030426
42337CB00016B/2413